MW00893237

For My Son

For My Son

Guided Journal

www.laquandamovemeant.com

ISBN-10: 1542317282
ISBN-13: 978-542317283

Table of Contents

Journal Guide

Here are 3 things you should know about the Journal:

1. Although this is a guided journal, you can leave any type of lessons you would like to leave for you child.

2. Just in case you don't know where to start, in the beginning of each section there are a list of questions that a child may have for a parent. You can start writing your lessons based on those questions or simply make up your own.

3. For the pages labeled *Encouraging Words | Funny Stories:*

   These pages are available for you to give a true story from your personal life that relates to the topic at hand or for you to simply provide your child some encouraging words that will help motivate them during their journey through life.

Happy Journaling!

These lessons are not designed to dictate how you should live your life, instead they are a guide to help along your way.

LESSONS ABOUT

LOVE

&

Relationships

MARRIAGE

AT WHAT AGE SHOULD I LOSE MY VIRGINITY?
HOW OLD SHOULD I BE WHEN I START DATING?
WHEN DO I LEAVE AN ABUSIVE RELATIONSHIP?
HOW DO I KNOW WHEN I'VE FOUND THE ONE?

LOVE OR MONEY?

HOW TO TELL IF SHE IS A GOLD DIGGER?
SHOULD I DATE SOMEONE WHO HAS A DIFFERENT FAITH THAN ME?
HOW TO RECOGNIZE IF SOMEONE IS ATTRACTED TO YOU?
SHOULD I SLEEP WITH THEM ON THE FIRST DATE?
SHOULD I STAY MARRIED OR IN A RELATIONSHIP FOR THE SAKE OF THE KIDS?
SHOULD WE LIVE TOGETHER BEFORE MARRIAGE?
SHOULD I DATE SOMEONE WITH CHILDREN?
HOW OLD SHOULD I BE BEFORE I GET MARRIED?
HOW LONG SHOULD I PURSUE HER?
SHOULD I MARRY FOR LOOKS?
WHAT SHOULD I LOOK FOR IN A GIRL?
WHAT IF RELATIONSHIPS AREN'T FOR ME?
SHOULD I PAY FOR THE FIRST DATE?
HOW DO I APPROACH A GIRL I'M INTERESTED IN?

Lesson 1: ____

Date: ________________

Lesson 2: ____

Date: ____________

Lesson 3: ______________________________

Date: ____________

Lesson 4: ____

Date: ____________

Lesson 5: ______________________________

Date: ____________

Lesson 6: ______________________________

Date: __________

Lesson 7: ____

Date: ____________

Lesson 8: ______________________________

Date: __________

Lesson 9: ____

Date: ____________

Lesson 10: ____________________

Date: __________

Lesson 11: ______________________________

Date: ____________

Lesson 12: ______________________________

Date: ____________

Lesson 13: ____

Date: ______________

Lesson 14: ____________________

Date: __________

Lesson 15: ____

Date: ____________

Lesson 16: ____

Date: ____________

Lesson 17: ______________________________________

Date: __________

Lesson 18: ______________________________

Date: __________

Lesson 19: ______________________________

Date: ____________

Lesson 20: ______________________________

Date: ___________

Lesson 21: ____

Date: ____________

Lesson 22: ____

Date: ____________

LESSONS ABOUT

Friendship

SHOULD I TRUST MY FRIENDS?
SHOULD I BE RIDE OR DIE FOR MY FRIENDS?
SHOULD I DATE MY FRIENDS EX?
IS BLOOD THICKER THAN WATER?
AGREEING TO DISAGREE?
HOW TO RECOGNIZE REAL FRIENDSHIPS?
WHAT IS TOO FRIENDLY?
HOW TO DO I MAKE NEW FRIENDS?
HOW DO I CUT OFF UNHEALTHY FRIENDSHIPS?
PEER PRESSURE?
What is a real friend?
SHOULD I CHANGE TO BE MORE LIKE MY FRIENDS?
AM I WEIRD FOR NOT HAVING ANY FRIENDS?
WHAT TO DO IF MY FRIEND IS TALKING ABOUT ME BEHIND MY BACK?
WHAT IF ME AND MY FRIEND LIKE THE SAME PERSON?
CAN I HAVE FRIENDS OF THE OPPOSITE SEX?
CAN I HAVE FRIENDS OF THE OPPOSITE SEX WHILE I'M IN A RELATIONSHIP?

Lesson 1: ____________________

Date: ____________

Lesson 2: ____

Date: ______________

Lesson 3: ______________________________

Date: __________

Lesson 4: ____________________

Date: ____________

Lesson 5: ____________________

Date: __________

Lesson 6: ______________________________

Date: ____________

Lesson 7: ____

Date: ____________

Lesson 8: ____

Date: ____________

Lesson 9: ____________________

Date: __________

Lesson 10: ____

Date: ____________

Lesson 11: ____

Date: ____________

Lesson 12: ____

Date: ____________

Lesson 13: ____

Date: ____________

Lesson 14: ______________________________

Date: __________

Lesson 15: ____

Date: ____________

Lesson 16: ______________________________

Date: ____________

LESSONS ABOUT

FAMILY

DO I ALWAYS HAVE TO FORGIVE MY FAMILY?

SIBLING RIVALRY?

IS BLOOD THICKER THAN WATER?

DO I HAVE TO LIKE ALL OF MY FAMILY MEMBERS?

SHOULD I EXPECT MY FAMILY MEMBERS TO NEVER HURT ME?

Should I expect family to help me every time I need help?

DO YOU LIKE MY OTHER SIBLINGS MORE THAT YOU LIKE ME?

SHOULD I EVER CUT MY FAMILY MEMBERS OFF?

Lesson 1: ____

Date: ____________

Lesson 2: ____________________

Date: ____________

Lesson 3: ____

Date: ____________

Lesson 4: ____

Date: ____________

Lesson 5: ____

Date: ____________

Lesson 6: ______________________________

Date: __________

Lesson 7: ____

Date: ____________

Lesson 8: ______________________________

Date: __________

LESSONS ABOUT

FAITH

IS GOD REAL?

CAN I HEAR GOD SPEAKING?

WHAT IF I WANT TO CHANGE MY FAITH?

Who is God?

WHAT BOOKS SHOULD I READ?

AM I ONLY ALLOWED TO BELIEVE WHAT YOU BELIEVE?

Lesson 1: ____

Date: ____________

Lesson 2: ____

Date: ____________

Lesson 3: ______________________________

Date: ____________

Lesson 4: ____

Date: ____________

Lesson 5: ______________________________

Date: __________

Lesson 6: ____

Date: ____________

LESSONS ABOUT

MONEY & CREDIT

SHOULD I LEND FAMILY MEMBERS MONEY?

SHOULD I LEND MY FRIENDS MONEY?

SHOULD I EVER PUT ANY BILL IN MY NAME FOR ANY FRIEND OR FAMILY MEMBER?

(E.G. CAR NOTE, MORTGAGE, ELECTRIC OR GAS)

SHOULD I GET A WILL?

SHOULD I SAVE FOR RETIREMENT AND WHEN?

SHOULD I GET LIFE INSURANCE?

WHAT IS CREDIT?

SHOULD I BUY OR LEASE MY CAR?

HOW MAY CREDIT CARDS SHOULD I HAVE?

IPHONE OR ANDROID?

SHOULD I HAVE A SEPARATE BANK ACCOUNT WHEN I'M MARRIED?

SHOULD I SPLIT THE BILLS WITH MY SPOUSE/GIRLFRIEND?

SHOULD I PAY ALL THE BILLS IN MY HOUSEHOLD?

SHOULD I GET CREDIT CARDS WHILE I'M IN COLLEGE?

How often should I give to those in need?

IS IT RIGHT TO GIVE UNTIL I HAVE NOTHING LEFT?

Lesson 1: ________________________________

Date: ____________

Lesson 2: ______________________________

Date: ____________

Lesson 3: ____

Date: ____________

Lesson 4: ______________________________

Date: __________

Lesson 5: ______________________________

Date: __________

Lesson 6: ____

Date: ____________

LESSONS ABOUT

Career

SHOULD I GO TO COLLEGE?
SHOULD I START MY OWN BUSINESS?
I LOVE DOING THIS THING! WHAT IF IT CAN'T FINANCIALLY SUPPORT ME?
LOVE OR MONEY?
SHOULD I PURSUE MY DREAMS OR JUST WORK A 9-5?
SHOULD I QUIT MY JOB AND FIND ANOTHER ONE?
IS IT OKAY TO RELOCATE?
HOW LONG SHOULD I PURSUE A GOAL BEFORE I GIVE UP?
HOW DO I DECIDE WHICH CAREER PATH TO CHOOSE?
WHAT AM I GOOD AT?
WHAT HAVE I ALWAYS LIKED TO DO?
WHAT DID YOU IMAGINE I WOULD BECOME?
IS IT EVER TOO LATE TO START A NEW JOB, GOAL OR DREAM?
WHAT ARE YOUR BIGGEST REGRETS ABOUT YOUR CAREER OR GOAL CHOICES?
WHAT ARE SOME OF YOUR GREATEST ACCOMPLISHMENTS?
HOW TO DISCOVER MY PURPOSE?
GOOD MOTIVATION TECHNIQUES TO KEEP MOVING FORWARD?
HOW TO CLIMB THE CORPORATE LADDER?
SHOULD I PURSUE A *creative* CAREER?
HELP! I DON'T HAVE ANY GOALS OR AMBITIONS?
I want to be a stay at home dad. Is that okay?

Lesson 1: ______________________________

Date: __________

Lesson 2: ______________________________

Date: __________

Lesson 3: ____

Date: __________

Lesson 4: ______________________________

Date: __________

Lesson 5: ____________________

Date: __________

Lesson 6: ____________________

Date: __________

Lesson 7: ______________________________

Date: ____________

Lesson 8: ______________________________

Date: ____________

Lesson 9: ____

Date: ______________

Lesson 10: ______________________________

Date: __________

Lesson 11: ______________________

Date: __________

Lesson 12: ____

Date: ____________

Lesson 13: ______________________________

Date: __________

Lesson 14: ____

Date: ____________

LESSONS ABOUT

RAISING YOUR OWN CHILDREN

TIME OUT OR BELT?
PUBLIC OR PRIVATE SCHOOL?
STEP PARENTING?
WHEN DO I TAKE MY CHILD TO THE ER?
WHAT'S A GOOD BED TIME?
HOW DO I BALANCE HAVING A CHILD/CHILDREN AND MY PERSONAL LIFE?
WHEN SHOULD I START SAVING FOR THEIR COLLEGE EDUCATION?
WHAT AGE ARE THEY ALLOWED TO SPEND THE NIGHT OVER SOMEONE ELSE'S HOUSE?
WHAT IS A GOOD PUNISHMENT?
PUBLIC OR PRIVATE SCHOOLS?
IS CULTURE AND HERITAGE IMPORTANT?
WHAT IS A GOOD PARENT?
WHAT IS A GOOD AGE FOR MY CHILD TO START DATING?
WHAT AGE SHOULD I ALLOW MY CHILD TO WEAR MAKE-UP?
WHEN DO I HAVE THE TALK ABOUT SEX?
HOW DO I HELP MY CHILD DISCOVER THEIR PURPOSE?
HOW TO NOT BE A CONTROLLING PARENT?

BALANCE?

Lesson 1: ______________________________

Date: ____________

Lesson 2: ____

Date: ____________

Lesson 3: ____

Date: ____________

Lesson 4: ______________________________

Date: __________

Lesson 5: ______________________________

Date: __________

Lesson 6: ______________________________

Date: ____________

Lesson 7: ______________________________

Date: __________

Lesson 8: ____________________

Date: ____________

OTHER VALUABLE LESSONS ABOUT LIFE

WHAT IS SELF LOVE?
SHOULD I EVER GET INTO A FIST FIGHT?
HEALTHY COMMUNICATION?
AGREEING TO DISAGREE?
SHOULD I PUT OFF GOING TO COLLEGE?
WHAT SHOULD I DO WHEN THINGS DON'T GO MY WAY?
WHAT IF I FEEL LIKE GIVING UP?
DEALING WITH INSECURITY?
JEALOUSY?
PRIDE VERSUS HUMILITY?
AM I UGLY?
HANDLING PEOPLES NEGATIVE OPINION ABOUT ME?
BREAKING BAD HABITS?
HOW TO HANDLE CONSTRUCTIVE CRITICISM?
HOW DO YOU SEE ME?
WHAT AM I GOOD AT?
WHAT IF NOBODY LIKE ME?
HOW TO HANDLE BULLIES?
HOW TO HANDLE REJECTION?
Do you love me?
RESPECTING MY ELDERS?
HEALTH AND WELLNESS?
RECOVERING FROM DISAPPOINTMENT OR LOSS?
STANDING FOR WHAT I BELIEVE IN?
HOW TO BECOME SUCCESSFUL?
CONFLICT RESOLUTION?

Lesson 1: ____

Date: ____________

Lesson 2: ____________________

Date: __________

Lesson 3: ____________________

Date: ____________

Lesson 4: ____

Date: ____________

Lesson 5: ______________________________

Date: __________

Lesson 6: ____

Date: ____________

Lesson 7: ____________________

Date: __________

Lesson 8: ______________________________

Date: __________

Lesson 9: ______________________________________

Date: ____________

Lesson 10: ____

Date: ____________

Lesson 11: ______________________________

Date: __________

Lesson 12: ______________________________

Date: __________

Lesson 13: ____

Date: ____________

Lesson 14: ______________________________

Date: __________

Lesson 15: ______________________________

Date: __________

Lesson 17: ____

Date: ______________

Lesson 19: ______________________________

Date: ____________

Lesson 20: ____

Date: ____________

Thank you for using this journal.

Please be sure to visit www.laquandamovemeant.com for other Guided Journals and Inspiration books!

Made in the USA
Monee, IL
11 July 2020

36433396R00105